Carol,

I am forever grateful to have met you at this time of my life.

♡ Dana

THE LITTLE BOOK OF
GRATITUDE

THE LITTLE BOOK OF
GRATITUDE

Bonnie Louise Kuchler

◪ WILLOW CREEK PRESS®

Published by Willow Creek Press, Inc.
P.O. Box 147, Minocqua, Wisconsin 54548

Photo Credits:

p2 © H. Schmidt-Roeger/KimballStock; p5 © Deb Garside /age fotostock;
p6 © Andrew Walmsley/NPL/Minden Pictures; p9 © Jan Vermeer/Foto Natura/Minden Pictures;
p10 © Marten Dalfors/age fotostock; p13 © Don Johnston/age fotostock; p14 © Mitsuaki Iwago/Minden Pictures;
p17 © Wildlife Bildagentur GmbH/KimballStock; p18 © Hiroya Minakuchi/Minden Pictures;
p21 © Klein-Hubert/KimballStock; p22 © S&D&K Maslowski/FLPA/Minden Pictures;
p25 © Mark Taylor/NPL/Minden Pictures; p26 George Sanker/NPL/Minden Pictures;
p29 © Claus Meyer/Minden Pictures; p30 © Mitsuaki Iwago/Minden Pictures;
p33 © Steven Kazlowski/NPL/Minden Pictures; p34 © Jack Milchanowski/age fotostock;
p37 © ZSSD/Minden Pictures; p38 © Peter Blackwell/NPL/Minden Pictures; p41 © Steven Kazlowski/KimballStock;
p42 © Anup Shah/NPL/Minden Pictures; p45 © Ferrero-Labat/Auscape/Minden Pictures;
p46 © Ron Kimball/KimballStock; p49 © Jurgen & Christine Sohns/FLPA/Minden Pictures;
p50 © Mark Taylor/NPL/Minden Pictures; p53 © Mark J. Barrett/KimballStock;
p54 © HPH Image Library/KimballStock; p57 © Winfried Wisniewski/FLPA/Minden Pictures;
p58 © Jurgen & Christine Sohns/FLPA/Minden Pictures;
p61 © John Eveson/FLPA/Minden Pictures; p62 © Jan Vermeer/Foto Natura/Minden Pictures;
p65 © Andy Rouse/NPL/Minden Pictures; p66 © Mitsuaki Iwago/Minden Pictures;
p69 © Michael Durham/Minden Pictures; p70 © Tui De Roy/Minden Pictures; p73 © Corbis/age fotostock;
p74 © Nick Upton/NPL/Minden Pictures; p77 © Terry Whittaker/2020VISION/Minden Pictures;
p78 © Anup Shah/NPL/Minden Pictures; p81 © Juniors Bildarchiv/age fotostock;
p82 © Kim Taylor/NPL/Minden Pictures; p85 © Jean Michel Labat/age fotostock;
p86 © Jane Burton/ NPL/Minden Pictures; p89 © P Mette/Blickwinkel/age fotostock;
p90 © Philip Lee Harvey/Cultúra RM/age fotostock; p93 © Yoshio Tomii/KimballStock;
p94 © Matthias Breiter/Minden Pictures

Design: Donnie Rubo
Printed in China

Words that express our deepest feelings—
like thankfulness—don't come easily.

Surely there's something more
impressive in the dictionary
than a lame "thank you!"
It doesn't begin to express
what I feel about you...

—Margot Thomson

The problem is,
there are no words that can jump off the page
and give you a hug.

Feeling gratitude and not expressing it
is like wrapping a present and not giving it.

—William Arthur Ward

So many times I've started thank-you
letters to you in my head.

Where do the unsaid thank you's go,
thank you's never spoken, but truly,
deeply felt?

—Chris Shea

When I think of you,
grateful feelings bubble to the surface.

Piglet noticed that even though he had a Very Small Heart,
it could hold a rather large amount of Gratitude.

—A. A. Milne

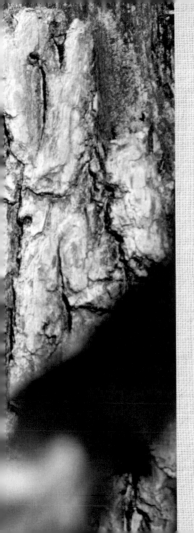

I can't hold these thank-you's
inside any longer.

I feel a very unusual sensation.
If it is not indigestion, I think it must be gratitude.

—Benjamin Disraeli

Do you ever wonder if anyone notices the caring things you do?

Looking back, we remember the clever,
the ingenious, the spectacular—
but most of all, we remember the kind.

—Pamela Dugdale

When I look over my life,
every high spot in the road
was because someone like you gave me a boost.

The low points came
when I tried to go it alone.

Thank you
for taking the time to be kind.
For thinking of me,
when it would have been easier
to think of yourself.

Many are called but few get up.

—Oliver Herford

Thank you
for making me feel special.

People touch our lives,
if only for a moment;
and yet we're not the same
from that moment on.

—Fern Bork

Thank you
for lending a hand when I felt overwhelmed.

What the heart gives away is never gone.
It is kept in the hearts of others.

—Robin St. John

Thank you
for propping me up when I needed someone to lean on.

Sometimes our light goes out
but is blown again into flame
by an encounter with another
human being. Each of us owes the
deepest thanks to those who have
rekindled this inner light.

—Albert Schweitzer

Thank you
for caring enough to listen.

One person who is truly understanding,
who takes the trouble to listen to us, can
change our whole outlook on the world.

—Elton Mayo

Thank you
for understanding when I've had a slip of the tongue.

What people really need is a good listening to.

—Mary Lou Casey

Thank you
for saying what needed to be said,
even if I didn't want to hear it.

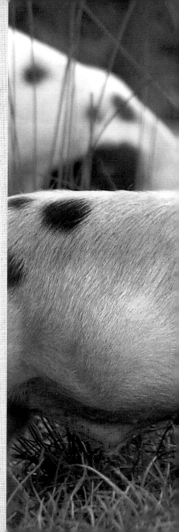

A word of kindness is
better than a fat pie.

—Russian proverb

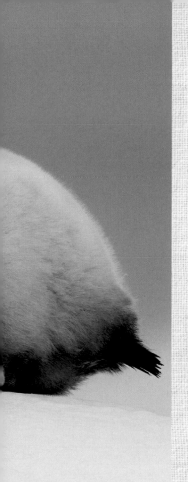

Thank you
for trying to see from my point of view.

There are people who take the heart out of you,
and there are people who put it back.

—Elizabeth David

Thank you
for that little push...
I needed it.

There are no little things.
Little things are the hinges of the universe.

—Fanny Fern

Thank you
for helping me find my way.

Too often we underestimate the power of a touch,
a smile, a kind word... or the smallest act of caring,
all of which have the potential to turn a life around.

—Felice Leonardo "Leo" Buscaglia

Thank you
for being there
when things didn't go as I had planned.

Those who bring sunshine into
the lives of others cannot keep
it from themselves.

—James Matthew Barrie

Thank you
for caring enough
to not let me feel sorry for myself.

Let us be grateful to the people
who make us happy; they are the charming
gardeners who make our souls blossom.

—Valentin Louis Georges Eugène Marcel Proust

Thank you
for putting a bounce in my step.

Gratitude is the song my heart
plays, when a hand of kindness
has plucked its strings.

—BLK

Thank you
for watching my back.

The greatest gift of life is friendship,
and I have received it.

—Hubert H. Humphrey

I can no other answer make, but
thanks, and thanks, and ever thanks.

—William Shakespeare

Thank you
for doing what no one else could do...
Thanks for being you.

Thank you most of all for
being there when I needed a friend.